Low Carb Vegetarian Recipes

The Ultimate Collection Of Super Natural Ketogenic Diet Recipes

Kaylee LOPEZ

TABLE OF CONTENTS

Steamed artichoke and garlic butter

Preparation Time: 15 minutes

Cooking Time: 15 Minutes Serving: 1

INGREDIENTS

- 1 artichoke
- 1/2 stick butter
- 1 clove garlic

DIRECTIONS

1. Wash the artichoke in cool water. Utilizing a serrated blade, put off the exceptional 1/4 of the artichoke
2. Trim the stem with the goal that it is around 1/2-inch lengthy and the artichoke stands upstanding.
3. Realize half of inch water to bubble in a pot massive enough to keep your artichoke.

4. When effervescent, include the artichoke and reduce warmth to a stew.

5. Cover and cook for around 30-40mins.

6. At the point when prepared, the artichoke has to extend in shading and a blade has to input the center without obstruction.

7. While your artichoke is steaming, set up the garlic unfold. Spot the spread in a skillet until completely softened. Include the garlic and mix it till aromatic.

8. Serve right away with a variety of napkins and an extra plate to position your leaf closes.

9. To devour an artichoke, pull off a leaf, dunk the bottom into the garlic margarine, and afterward scratch the buttered tissue off together with your teeth.

NUTRITION: Calories: 454, Fat 31g, Carbs 26g, Sugars 4.4g, Protein 22g

Acorn Squash Slices

Preparation Time: 15 minutes

Cooking Time: 40 Minutes

Serving: 6

INGREDIENTS

- 2 medium acorn squash
- 1/2 teaspoon salt
- 3/4 cup maple syrup
- 2 tablespoons butter
- 1/3 cup chopped pecans

DIRECTIONS

1. Cut squash down the middle longwise; evacuate and dispose of seeds and film. Cut every half widthwise into 1/2-in. cuts; dispose of finishes.

2. Spot cuts in a lubed 13-in. x 9-in. preparing dish. Sprinkle with salt. Join syrup and spread; pour over squash. Sprinkle with walnuts whenever wanted.

3. Cover and prepare at 350° for 40-45 minutes or until delicate.

NUTRITION: Calories 170, Fat 7g, Carbs 31g, Sugars 0.2g, Protein 2g

Keto Parsley Cauliflower Rice

Preparation Time: 10minutes

Cooking Time: 10 Minutes Serving: 2

INGREDIENTS

- 1 head cauliflower washed and dried
- 1 tablespoon olive oil
- 2 cloves garlic and Pinch cayenne
- 1/3 cup parsley
- salt and ground black pepper

DIRECTIONS

1. Dispose of the leaves and reduce a medium-sized cauliflower head in quarters and mesh each one in every one of them using a container grater with medium openings.
2. On the occasion that you need to secure your arms at some stage in grinding, a first-rate approach to accomplish that is to make use of cut secure gloves.
3. Warmth a drag of olive oil in a large skillet. Sautée minced garlic till outstanding.
4. Include cauliflower rice, mix and unfold with a top. Cook for around 10 minutes, blending on more than one

occasion.

5. Include hacked parsley, salt, dark pepper and a gap of cayenne. Appreciate!

NUTRITION: Calories: 141, Fat 7g, Carbs 15g, Sugar 5g, Protein 6g

Sautéed Radishes with Green Beans

Preparation Time: 10 minutes

Cooking Time: 10 Minutes Serving: 4

INGREDIENTS

- 1 tablespoon butter
- 1/2 pound fresh green
- 1 cup thinly sliced radishes
- 1/2 teaspoon sugar and 1/4 tsp salt
- 2 tsps pine nuts

DIRECTIONS

1. In an enormous skillet, heat spread over medium-high warmth. Include beans;

cook and mix 3-4 minutes or until fresh delicate.

2. Include radishes; cook 2-3 minutes longer or until vegetables are delicate, mixing once in a while. Mix in sugar and salt; sprinkle with nuts.

NUTRITION: Calories 75, Fat 6g, Carbs 5g, Sugars 2g, Protein 2g

Sweet Potato & Bean Quesadillas

Preparation Time: 15 minutes

Cooking Time: 15 Minutes Serving: 4

INGREDIENTS

- 2 medium sweet potatoes
- 4 whole-wheat tortillas
- 3/4 cup canned black beans
- 1/2 cup shredded pepper jack cheese
- 3/4 cup salsa

DIRECTIONS

1. Clean sweet potatoes; penetrate a few times with a fork. Spot on a microwave- safe plate. Microwave, revealed, on high, turning once, until delicate, 7-9mints

2. At the point when cool enough to deal with, cut every potato the long way down the middle. Scoop out the mash. Spread onto half of every tortilla; top with beans and cheddar. Crease another portion of tortilla packing.

3. Warmth a cast-iron skillet or frying pan over medium warmth, cook quesadillas until brilliant darker and cheddar are dissolved, 2-3 minutes on each side. Present with salsa.

NUTRITION: Calories 306, Fat 8g, Carb 46g, Sugars 9g, Protein 11g

Toasted Ravioli Puffs

Preparation Time: 15 minutes

Cooking Time: 15 Minutes

Serving: 2 dozen

INGREDIENTS

- 24 refrigerated cheese ravioli
- 1 tsp reduced-fat Italian salad dressing
- 1 tsp Italian-style panko bread
- 1 tsp grated Parmesan cheese
- Warm marinara sauce

DIRECTIONS

1. Preheat broiler to 400°. Cook ravioli as per bundle headings; channel. Move to a lubed heating sheet.
2. Brush with serving of mixed greens dressing. In a little bowl, blend bread morsels and cheddar; sprinkle over ravioli.
3. Heat 12-15 minutes or until brilliant dark- colored. Present with marinara sauce.

NUTRITION: Calories 21, Fat 1g, Carbs 3g, Sugars 0.2g, Protein 1g

Tomato & Avocado Sandwiches

Preparation Time: 5 minutes

Cooking Time: 5 Minutes Serving: 2

INGREDIENTS

- 1/2 medium ripe avocado
- 4 slices whole-wheat bread
- 1 medium tomato
- 2 tsps shallot
- 1/4 cup hummus

DIRECTIONS

1.Spread avocado more than two cuts of toast. Top with tomato and shallot. Spread hummus over residual toast; place over avocado toast.

NUTRITION: Calories 278, Fat 11g, Carbs 35g, Sugars 6g, Protein 11g

Apple, White Cheddar & Arugula Tarts

Preparation Time: 15 minutes

Cooking Time: 15 Minutes Serving: 4

INGREDIENTS

- 1 sheet frozen puff pastry
- 1 cup shredded white cheddar cheese
- 2 medium apples
- 2 tsps olive oil and 1 tsp lemon juice
- 3 cups fresh arugula

DIRECTIONS

1. Preheat stove to 400°. On a daintily floured surface, unfurl puff baked good; fold into a 12-in. square. Cut baked goods into four squares; place on a material paper-lined heating sheet.

2. Sprinkle half of each square with cheddar to inside 1/4 in. of edges; top with apples. Crease baked good packing.

3. Press edges with a fork to seal. Heat 16- 18 minutes or until brilliant darker.

4. In a bowl, whisk oil and lemon juice until mixed; add arugula and remove to cover. Present with tarts.

NUTRITION: Calories 518, Fat 33g, Carbs 46g, Sugars 8g, Protein 12g

Risotto Cakes

Preparation Time: 15 minutes

Cooking Time: 15 Minutes Serving: 4

INGREDIENTS

- 1 large egg
- 2 cups cold leftover risotto
- 1 cup coarse -wheat breadcrumbs
- 2 teaspoons extra-virgin olive oil

DIRECTIONS

1. Beat egg in an enormous bowl; mix in risotto and ½ cup breadcrumbs. Spot the remaining ½ cup breadcrumbs in a shallow dish. Structure the risotto blend into eight 2½-inch cakes and dig in the breadcrumbs.

2. Coat an enormous nonstick skillet with cooking shower;

include 1 teaspoon oil and warmth over medium warmth. Include the cakes and cook until caramelized on the main site, 2 to 4 minutes.

3. To make your very own breadcrumbs, trim outsides from entire wheat bread. Attack pieces and procedure in a nourishment processor until coarse scraps structure

4. Spread on a heating sheet and prepare at 250°F until dry, around 10 to 15 minutes.

5. For locally acquired coarse dry breadcrumbs, we like Ian's image, marked "Panko breadcrumbs." Find them at well- supplied grocery stores.

NUTRITION: Calories 303, Fat 9g, Carb 40g, Sugar 0.2g, Protein 11g

Pan Seared Duck Breast

Preparation Time: 15 minutes

Cooking Time: 20 Minutes Serving: 2

INGREDIENTS

- 1 medium duck breast
- Salt and pepper to taste

DIRECTIONS

1. Remove the duck bosom from the ice chest and pat it genuine dry. Score the skin in a mismatched design with a sharp edge. This will help discharge the fat that is situated under the skin and will likewise bring about a crispier skin.

2. Sprinkle the duck bosom liberally with salt and pepper, at that point place it skin side down in a chilly, dry skillet. Truly, it's hard to believe, but it's true. No compelling reason to preheat the dish or add fat to it. Beginning with a virus dish will guarantee that we get the most fat to render. Turn the warmth up to medium-

   high and cook the duck bosom until the skin turns out to be wonderfully brilliant dark-colored, slight and fresh, which should take around 6-8 minutes, contingent upon the underlying thickness of the skin.

3. Turn the bosom over and cook for an extra 3 to 5 minutes for uncommon to medium-uncommon (interior temperature should peruse 125°F – 130°F on moment read thermometer.

4. Remove the duck from the container and let it lay on a cutting board, skin side up for around 5 minutes. Much the same as a decent steak, a duck bosom needs to rest, generally.

5. Cut with cuts cut on the inclination and on the corner to corner and serve.

NUTRITION: Calories 460, Fat 36g, Carbs 0.2g, Sugars 0.4g, Protein 34g

Creamy Mushroom and Cauliflower Risotto Recipe

Preparation Time: 20 minutes Cooking
Time: 15 Minutes Serving: 5

INGREDIENTS

- Cauliflower
- Garlic Cloves
- Sliced Mushrooms
- 1/4 to 1/2 cup Liquid
- Butter/Coconut Oil

DIRECTIONS

1. 1 Rice the cauliflower either in a nourishment processor or with a container grater.
2. 2 Warmth a little coconut oil or spread in a skillet over medium to high warmth
3. 3 At the point when hot, include the garlic and mushrooms.
4. 4 Saute until diminished.
5. 5 Include the cauliflower and your fluid of decision.
6. 6 Stew delicately, mixing normally until the cauliflower is cooked through.

NUTRITION: Calories: 460, Fat 38g, Carbs 3g, Sugar 1g, Protein 27g

Grilled Halloumi Brochette

Preparation Time: 10minutes Cooking

Time: 10 Minutes; Servings: 12 slices

INGREDIENTS

- 2 medium tomatoes

- 1/4 cup chopped fresh basil

- 2 to 3 cloves garlic

- 2 tbsp olive oil, Salt, and pepper

- 2 7- ounce packages Halloumi cheese

DIRECTIONS

1. 1 In an enormous, consolidate tomatoes, basil, garlic, olive oil, salt, and pepper. Blend well and refrigerate

2. 2 Cut each bit of halloumi once transversely and afterward cut into even 1/2 inch to 1/2-inch slender cuts.

3. 3 You will get around 12 cuts of cheddar. Barbecue over medium warmth until flame broil marks show up on the cheddar, around 2 to 3 minutes for every side. You should relax the cheddar with a metal spatula to turn.

4. 4 Move to a serving platter and top with tomato basil blend.

NUTRITION: Calories 134, Fat 11.24g, Carbs 0.96g, Sugar 0.26g, Protein 7.24g

Moroccan Roasted Green Beans

Preparation Time: 20 minutes

Cooking Time: 25 Minutes Serving: 4

INGREDIENTS

- cups raw green beans
- 1 tsp kosher salt
- 1/2 tsp ground black pepper
- 1 Tbsp Rasel Hangout seasoning
- 2 Tbsp olive oil

DIRECTIONS   :

5. 1 Remove the green beans, olive oil, and seasonings collectively and spread out on a great treat sheet or broiling skillet.
6. 2 Cook at 400 levels (F for 20 minutes.
7. 3 Remove from the broiler and blend.
8. 4 Come lower back to the broiler and dish an extra 10 minutes.
9. 5 Remove and serve heat or chilled.

NUTRITION: Calories 73, Fat 5g, Carbs 4g, Sugar 2g, Protein 8g

Caprese Style Portobello's

Preparation Time: 15 minutes

Cooking Time: 20 Minutes Serving: 4

INGREDIENTS

- Large Portobello mushroom caps
- Cherry tomatoes
- Shredded or fresh mozzarella
- Fresh basil
- Olive oil

DIRECTIONS   :

1. 1 Warmth stove to four hundred levels
2. 2 Line a getting ready sheet with foil for simple cleanup.
3. 3 Brush the tops and edges with olive oil on every mushroom.
4. 4 Cut cherry or grape tomatoes down the middle, area in a bowl, sprinkle with olive oil, and encompass cleaved basil, salt, and pepper.
5. 5 Give it a danger to take a seat for multiple moments to permit them to flavors merge.
6. 6 Spot your cheddar on the bottom of the mushroom

top, spoon at the tomato basil blend and put together until cheddar melts and mushrooms are cooked but not overcooked.

NUTRITION: Calories: 520, Fat 41g, Carbs 0.5g, Sugar 0.2g, Protein 41g

Egg Nest Recipe with Braised Cabbage

Preparation Time: 2minutes

Cooking Time: 7 Minutes Serving: 2

INGREDIENTS

- 1 teaspoon ghee

- 4 cups cabbage shredded

- 1/8 teaspoon salt

- 1 tablespoon apple cider vinegar

- Pepper and 2 eggs

DIRECTIONS

1. Soften ghee in a huge griddle that has a fitted top over medium-high warmth.

2. Include cabbage and salt. Remove with the liquefied ghee.

3. Keep cooking over medium-high warmth until the cabbage tans, around 3- 4 minutes. Blend in apple juice vinegar and pepper.

4. Accumulate cabbage into two little hills. Utilizing the back of a spoon, structure a well in each hill to make space for the eggs

5. Break an egg into every space in the cabbage.

6. Decrease the warmth to low-medium and cook until whites of egg firm and yolk arrive at wanted consistency. Season with salt and pepper to taste

NUTRITION: Calories: 121, Fat 6g, Carbs 8g, Sugar 4g, Protein 7g

Eggs En Cocotte Recipe

Preparation Time: 10minutes

Cooking Time: 15 Minutes Serving: 3

INGREDIENTS

- 1 tablespoon ghee
- 2 cups mushrooms
- salt and 3 eggs
- 1 tablespoon chives
- 3 tablespoons heavy cream

DIRECTIONS

1. Utilizing the sauté putting of a multi- cooker, dissolve ghee, at that point sauté mushrooms together, until delicate, caramelized, and reduced to 3/4 cup. Season with salt to taste

2. In the intervening time, oil the ramekins. At the factor whilst mushrooms are cooked, separate into ramekins. Top every with a teaspoon of chives, a crisply cut up egg, and a tablespoon of cream

3. The multi-cooker pots are nonstick; accordingly you should not have to wash them. Essentially add 2 cups of

water to the bottom of the Instant Pot.

4. Include the trivet, and spot the egg- crammed ramekins on top. Verify and lock the duvet of the multi-cooker. Weight cook on low for 1-2mins

5. Fast discharge and directly evacuate the pinnacle whilst the burden has standardized. Cautiously remove the ramekins. They'll be warm, so use heatproof broiler gloves or artisan box lifters.

6. Present with newly toasted bread, just like pecan levain as imagined.

NUTRITION Fact: Calories: 113, Fat 6.9g, Carbs 6.8g, Sugar 4.3g, Protein 7.9g

Cheesy Garlic Roasted Asparagus

Preparation Time: 10minutes

Cooking Time: 20 Minutes Serving: 4-6

INGREDIENTS

- 1 pound asparagus spears
- 3 tsps olive oil
- 1 tsp minced garlic and 3/4 tsp kosher salt
- 1/4 tsp fresh cracked black pepper
- 1 1/4 cups mozzarella cheese

DIRECTIONS

1. Preheat broiler to 425°F. Delicately oil a preparing sheet with nonstick cooking oil shower.

2. 2Organize asparagus on the prepared sheet. Put in a safe spot.

3. 3In a little bowl combine olive oil, garlic, salt, and pepper

4. Sprinkle   the   oil   blend   over   the asparagus and remove to equally cover.

5. Top with mozzarella cheddar. Heat for 10-15 minutes until energetic and simply starting to get delicate, at that point sear until the cheddar gets brilliant

6. Change salt and pepper, if necessary. Serve right away.

NUTRITION: Calories: 440, Fat 48g, Carbs 0.2g Sugar 0.4g, Protein 4g

Asparagus + Goat cheese frittata

Preparation Time: 10 minutes

Cooking Time: 25 Minutes Serving: 4

INGREDIENTS

- 1/2 pound asparagus
- 12 eggs
- 2 Tablespoons milk or cream
- 2 to 4 ounces soft goat cheese
- Olive oil, black pepper, and 1/2 tsp salt

INSTRUCTIONS

1. Beat the eggs and trim and reduce the asparagus into scaled-down pieces. Cooperation makes fantasy paintings!

2. Toss the asparagus into the solid iron with some olive oil, season it with salt and pepper, and prepare dinner until softly roasted and sensitive, around 12-15 mins.

3. Empty the eggs into the cast iron, spreading them equitably. Cook them until they may be set round the rims.

4. Asparagus and Goat Cheese Frittata Camping Recipe

5. Sprinkle little bits of the goat cheddar round the very

best factor of the frittata.

6. Spread with tinfoil and prepare dinner for 15-20mins. Evacuate the tinfoil and permit the frittata sit down for round 5mins before slicing and serving.

NUTRITION: Calories: 321, Fat 9g, Carbs 14g, Sugar 4.1g, Protein 24g

Easy Vegetable Ratatouille

Preparation Time: 1 hour Servings 4

NUTRITION: 159 Calories; 10.4g Fat; 5.7g Carbs; 6.4g Protein; 5g Fiber

INGREDIENTS

- 1 large onion, sliced
- 1/3 cup Parmesan cheese, shredded
- 1 celery, peeled and diced
- 1 poblano pepper, minced
- 1 eggplant, cut into thick slices
- 1 cup grape tomatoes, halved
- 1/2 garlic head, minced
- 2 tablespoons extra-virgin olive oil
- 1 tablespoon fresh basil leaves, snipped

DIRECTIONS

1. Sprinkle the eggplant with 1 teaspoon of salt and let it stand for about 30 minutes; drain and rinse under running water.

2. Place the eggplant slices in the bottom of a lightly-oiled casserole dish. Add in the remaining vegetable. Add in the

olive oil and basil leaves.

3. Bake in the preheated oven at 350 degrees F for about 30 minute or until thoroughly cooked.

4. Storing

5. Place the vegetable ratatouille in airtight containers or Ziploc bags; keep in your refrigerator for up to 3 to 5 days.

6. To freeze, place the vegetable ratatouille in freezer storage bags. Freeze for up to

   12 months. Top with the cheese and place under the preheated broiler for 5 to 6 minutes. Bon appétit!

Champinones Al Ajillo with Keto Naan

Preparation Time: 20 minutes Servings 6

NUTRITION: 281 Calories; 21.4g Fat; 6.1g Carbs; 6.4g Protein; 1.4g Fiber

INGREDIENTS

- 1 pound button mushrooms, thinly sliced
- 1 teaspoon Spanish paprika
- 1/4 teaspoon flaky sea salt
- 8 tablespoons coconut oil, melted
- 1 egg plus 1 egg yolk, beaten
- 1/4 cup coconut flour
- 1/2 cup almond flour
- 1/2 teaspoon baking powder
- 2 tablespoons psyllium powder
- 1 tablespoon butter
- 1 teaspoon garlic, minced

DIRECTIONS

1. Mix the flour with the baking powder, psyllium and salt until well combined.

2. Add in 6 tablespoons of coconut oil, egg and egg yolk; pour in the water and stir to form a dough; let it stand for about 15 minutes.

3. Divide the dough into 6 pieces and roll them out to form a disc. Use the remaining 2 tablespoons of coconut oil to bake naan bread.

4. In a sauté pan, cook the mushrooms and garlic in hot butter until the mushrooms

release liquid; season with Spanish paprika. Taste and adjust seasonings.

5. Storing

6. Place the mushrooms in airtight containers; keep in your refrigerator for 3 to 5 days.

7. Place the naan bread in airtight containers; keep in your refrigerator for 3 to 5 days.

8. Place the mushrooms in a plastic freezer bags; they will maintain the best quality for 10 to 12 months.

Spring Mixed Greens Salad

Preparation Time: 10 minutes Servings 4

NUTRITION: 190 Calories; 17.6g Fat; 7.6g Carbs; 4.3g Protein; 3.9g Fiber

INGREDIENTS

- 1 cup romaine lettuce
- 1 cup lollo rosso
- 1/3 cup goat cheese, crumbled
- 2 tablespoons fresh parsley, chopped
- 2 tablespoons extra-virgin olive oil
- 1/2 lime, freshly squeezed
- 2 cups baby spinach
- 1/2 cup blueberries
- 1 cup avocado, pitted, peeled and sliced
- Sea salt and white pepper, to taste

DIRECTIONS

1. Toss all Ingredients in a mixing bowl. Taste and adjust seasonings.
2. Place in your refrigerator until ready to use.
3. Storing
4. Place the salad in airtight container or heavy-duty freezer bags; keep in the refrigerator for up to 3 to 4 days.

Aromatic Chinese Cabbage

Preparation Time: 15 minutes Servings 4

NUTRITION: 142 Calories; 11.6g Fat; 5.7g Carbs; 2g Protein; 1.8g Fiber

INGREDIENTS

- 4 tablespoons sesame oil
- 1 pound Chinese cabbage, outer leaves discarded, cored and shredded
- 1 tablespoon rice wine
- 1 celery rib, thinly sliced
- 1/4 teaspoon fresh ginger root, grated
- 1/2 teaspoon sea salt
- 1/2 cup onion, chopped
- 1 teaspoon garlic, pressed
- 1/2 teaspoon Sichuan pepper
- 1/4 cup vegetable stock

DIRECTIONS

1. In a wok, heat the sesame oil over a medium-high flame. Stir fry the onion, and garlic for 1 minute or until just tender and fragrant.

2. Add in the cabbage, celery, and ginger and continue to cook for 7 to 8 minutes more, stirring frequently to ensure even cooking.

3. Stir in the remaining Ingredients and continue to cook for a further 3 minutes.

4. Storing

5. Place the Chinese cabbage in airtight containers or Ziploc bags; keep in your refrigerator for up to 3 to 4 days.

6. For freezing, place the Chinese cabbage in airtight containers or heavy-duty freezer bags. Freeze up to 2 to 3 months. Defrost in the refrigerator. Bon appétit!

Vegan Keto Porridge

Preparation Time: 15 minutes

Cooking Time: 20 Minutes Serving: 4

INGREDIENTS

- 2 tablespoons coconut flour
- 3 tablespoons golden flaxseed meal
- 2 tablespoons vegan vanilla protein powder
- 1 ½ cups unsweetened almond milk
- Powdered erythritol

DIRECTIONS   :

1. In a bowl combine the coconut flour, brilliant flaxseed dinner, and protein powder.
2. Add to a pot, alongside the almond milk, and cook over medium warmth. It will appear to be exceptionally free from the start.
3. At the point when it thickens you can mix in your favored measure of sugar. I like to use about ½ a tablespoon. Present with your preferred garnishes.

NUTRITION: Calories 423, Fat 24g, Carbs 8g, Sugar 6g, Protein 24g

Cinnamon Faux-st Crunch Cereal

Preparation Time: 15 minutes

Cooking Time: 15 Minutes Serving: 4

INGREDIENTS

- 1/2 cup milled flax seed
- 1/2 cup hulled hemp seeds
- 2 Tbsp ground cinnamon
- 1/2 cup apple juice
- 1 Tbsp coconut oil

DIRECTIONS

1. Consolidate the dry Ingredients in a Magic Bullet, blender or nourishment processor. Include the squeezed apple and coconut oil and method until absolutely consolidated

2. Spread the participant out on a fabric coated treat sheet until first rate and flimsy – round 1/16 of an inch thick.

3. Heat in a preheated 300 degree (F broiler for 15mins, lower the warmth to 250 ranges (F and prepare for an additional 10 minutes.

4. Remove from the broiler and utilizing a pizza shaper or blade, reduce into squares about the scale of the keys on your PC console.

5. Mood killer the broiler and set the oat back internal for about 60mins or till it is fresh

6. Present with unsweetened almond or coconut milk

NUTRITION: Calories 129, Fat 9g, Carbs 1.3g, Sugar 1.1g, Protein 16g

Keto Muffins

Preparation Time: 5minutes

Cooking Time: 26 Minutes Serving: 12

<u>INGREDIENTS</u>

- 8 oz Cream Cheese
- 8 large eggs
- 4 tbsp Butter
- 2 scoops Whey Protein

<u>DIRECTIONS</u>

1. In a blending, bowl liquefies spread and cream cheddar.

2. Include whey protein and eggs, cautious not to cook the eggs from the warmth of the margarine.

3. Join with a hand blender until totally blended.

4. Fill biscuit preparing plate and heat at 350 degrees for 26 minutes. Appreciate!

NUTRITION: Calories 165.1, Fat 13.6g, Carbs 1.5g, Sugar 4g, Protein 9.6g

Caprese Grilled eggplant roll- ups

Preparation Time: 5minutes

Cooking Time: 8 Minutes Servings: 8 bites

INGREDIENTS

- 1 eggplant aubergine
- 4 oz mozzarella 115g
- 1 tomato large
- 2 basil leaves
- Good quality olive oil

DIRECTIONS

1. Ensure your blade is sharp before beginning. Cut the end of the eggplant at that point cut it in slim cuts, around 0.1in/0.25cm thick the long way. Dispose of the littler pieces that are mostly skin and not as long from either side.

2. Cut the mozzarella and tomato daintily too. Shred the basil leaves meagerly.

3. Warm a frying pan skillet and gently brush the eggplant cuts with olive oil. On the other hand, shower on a little and rapidly rub over before it is ingested. Spot the eggplant cuts on the skillet and flame broil for two or three minutes each side.

4. Top it with a cut of tomato, and include a little bit of mozzarella at the more slender end. Sprinkle over two or three bits of

basil and shower a little olive oil and two or three toils of dark pepper.

5. Roll the eggplant from the more slender end, which has just the cheddar.

NUTRITION: Calories: 59, Fat 3g, Carbs 4g, Sugar 2g, Protein 3g

Stuffed Zucchini with goat cheese & marinara

Preparation Time: 15 minutes Cooking
Time: 25 Minutes Serving: 4

INGREDIENTS

- 4 medium-sized zucchini
- 1 5- ounce log goat cheese
- 1-2 cups marinara sauce
- Chopped parsley

DIRECTIONS

1. Preheat range or flame broil to 400F.
2. Cut zucchini down the center the lengthy manner and scoop out the seeds, forgetting approximately the zucchini emptied.
3. Season with in shape salt and crisply ground dark pepper and see on a heating sheet
4. Utilizing half of of the goat cheddar, spread a modest quantity at the base of every zucchini.
5. Spoon marinara sauce on pinnacle, at that factor dab with super goat cheddar

6. Flame broil or put together till goat cheddar is sensitive and marinara is growing round 10 minutes. Serve right away.

NUTRITION: Calories: 412, Fat 22g, Carbs 17g, Sugar 4g, Protein 33g

Simple Greek Salad

Preparation Time: 20 minutes

Cooking Time: 15 Minutes Serving: 4

INGREDIENTS

- 2 cucumbers
- 1-pint grape tomatoes
- 4 oz feta cheese cubed
- 2 tbsp fresh dill
- 2 tbsp extra virgin olive oil

DIRECTIONS   :

1.Join the initial four Ingredients in a medium bowl. Sprinkle with the olive oil.

NUTRITION: Calories 118, Fat 9g, Carbs 7g, Sugars 4g, Protein 4.1g

Crunchy & Nutty Cauliflower Salad

Preparation Time: 15 minutes

Cooking Time: 15 Minutes Serving: 3

INGREDIENTS

- 3 cups cauliflower
- 1 cup leek
- 1/2 cup organic walnuts
- 1 cup full-fat sour cream
- unrefined sea salt OR Himalayan salt

INSTRUCTIONS

1. Consolidate all Ingredients in a huge bowl. Blend until very much blended.
2. Move into a sealed shut compartment.
3. Refrigerate at any rate 3 hours before serving with the goal that the flavors blend and get further.

NUTRITION: Calories: 571, Fat 44g, Carbs 2g, Sugar 2g, Protein 42g

Zucchini Noodles with Avocado Sauce

Preparation Time: 10 Minutes Serving: 2

INGREDIENTS

- 1 zucchini and 1 avocado
- 1 1/4 cup basil and 1/3 cup water
- 4 tbsp pine nuts
- 2 tbsp lemon juice
- 12 cherry tomatoes

DIRECTIONS   :

1. Make the zucchini noodles utilizing a peeler or the Spiralizer
2. Mix the remainder of the Ingredients in a blender until smooth.
3. Consolidate noodles, avocado sauce and cherry tomatoes in a blending bowl.
4. These zucchini noodles with avocado sauce are better new; however, you can store them in the cooler for 1 to 2 days.

NUTRITION: Calories: 313, Fat 26.8g, Carbs 18.7g, Sugar 6.5g, Protein 6.8g

Grain-Free Keto Granola

Preparation Time: 2minutes

Cooking Time: 20 Minutes Serving: 4

INGREDIENTS

- 1 cup nuts and seeds
- 1 tablespoon agave syrup
- 1/2 teaspoon vanilla extract
- 1 teaspoon almond extract
- 1 tablespoon coconut
- 1/4 cup coconut chips

DIRECTIONS   :

1. Preheat broiler to 325°.
2. Blend agave syrup, vanilla concentrate, almond concentrate, and coconut oil in a bowl. Warmth in microwave 20-30 seconds to consolidate.
3. Pour blend over nuts and seeds, and consolidate altogether. Heat at 325° for 10 minutes. Flip, and prepare 5 minutes. Include coconut chips and heat 5 minutes more.

NUTRITION: Calories: 299, Fat 8g, Carbs 14g, Sugar 4g, Protein 6g

Cheesy Ranch Roasted Broccoli

Preparation Time: 15 minutes

Cooking Time: 25 Minutes Serving: 3

INGREDIENTS

- 4 cups broccoli florets
- 1/4 cup ranch dressing
- 1/2 cup sharp cheddar cheese
- 1/4 cup heavy whipping cream
- kosher salt and pepper to taste

DIRECTIONS :

1. Remove the entirety of the Ingredients together in a medium-sized bowl until the broccoli is very much covered.

2. Spread out the broccoli blend in an 8 x 8 ovenproof goulash dish. Heat in a preheated stove at 375 degrees (F for 30 minutes

3. If not delicate enough for your inclination, place back in the broiler for another 5 – 10 minutes, or until wanted delicacy is come to. Serve hot.

NUTRITION: Calories 135, Fat 11g, Carbs 3g, Sugar 2g, Protein 4g

Keto Creamy Avocado Pasta with Shirataki

Preparation Time: 10 minutes Cooking

Time: 15 Minutes Serving: 4

INGREDIENTS

- packet of shirataki noodles
- avocado ripe
- 1/4- cup heavy cream
- tsp dried basil
- tsp black pepper and 1 tsp salt

DIRECTIONS   :

1. Set up the shirataki
2. Channel the shirataki noodles in a colander to remove the fluid they come bundled in. Wash completely under running water.
3. Heat up some water and cook the shirataki for 1-2mins to evacuate any waiting aroma.
4. Deplete and wash once more.
5. Warmth a perfect dry skillet and toss in the shirataki. The noodles contain a lot of water, so this will help dry them out to evacuate a portion of their coagulated surface.

NUTRITION: Calories: 453, Fat 42g, Carbs 16g, Sugar 3g, Protein 4g

Easy Zucchini Noodle Alfredo

Preparation Time: 12minutes

Cooking Time: 10 Minutes; Servings: 4

INGREDIENTS

- pound zucchini
- 1 Tablespoon olive oil
- ounces cream cheese
- 1 Tablespoon low-fat sour cream
- 1/4 cup Parmesan cheese grated

DIRECTIONS   :

1. 1 Utilize a spiralizer or vegetable peeler to made zucchini noodles.
2. 2 Warmth olive oil in a huge skillet over medium warmth
3. 3 Add zucchini noodles to the container and sauté for around 5 minutes.
4. 4 Remove noodles to serving the dish.
5. 5 Include cream cheddar, acrid cream, and Parmesan cheddar to the skillet and mix to join.
6. 6 Pour sauce over noodles and remove to consolidate.

7. 7 Top with extra Parmesan cheddar, whenever wanted.

NUTRITION: Calories: 100, Fat 7g, Carbs 4g, Sugar 3g, Protein 4g

Roasted Autumn Vegetables

Preparation Time: 35 minutes Servings 6

NUTRITION: 137 Calories; 11.1g Fat; 3.1g Carbs; 1.2g Protein; 2.3g Fiber

INGREDIENTS

- 3 tablespoons olive oil
- 1 onion, cut into wedges
- 1 fresh chili pepper, minced
- 1/2 pound celery, quartered
- 1/2 pound bell peppers, sliced
- 1/2 pound turnips, cut into wedges
- Sea salt and ground black pepper, to taste
- 1 teaspoon dried thyme
- 1 teaspoon dried basil

- 1 garlic clove, minced

DIRECTIONS

1. Toss all Ingredients in a roasting pan. Roast in the preheated oven at 410 degrees F for 30 minutes.
2. Taste and adjust the seasoning.
3. Storing
4. Place the roasted vegetables in airtight containers or Ziploc bags; keep in your refrigerator for up to 3 to 5 days.
5. To freeze, arrange the roasted vegetables on a baking sheet in a single layer; freeze for about 2 hours. Transfer the frozen fries to freezer storage bags. Freeze for up to 12 months. Bon appétit!

Easy Keto Coleslaw

Preparation Time: 10 minutes + chilling time Servings 4

NUTRITION: 242 Calories; 20.5g Fat; 6.2g Carbs; 1g Protein; 3.1g Fiber

INGREDIENTS

- 3/4 pound cabbage, cored and shredded
- 1/4 cup fresh cilantro, chopped
- 1/4 cup fresh chives, chopped
- 1 teaspoon fennel seeds
- Salt and pepper, to taste
- 1 large-sized celery, shredded
- 1 teaspoon deli mustard
- 2 tablespoons sesame seeds, lightly toasted
- 1 cup mayonnaise

DIRECTIONS

1. Toss the cabbage, celery, mayonnaise, mustard, cilantro, chives, fennel seeds, salt, and pepper in a bowl.
2. Sprinkle toasted sesame seeds over your salad.
3. Storing
4. Place the salad in airtight containers or Ziploc bags; keep in your refrigerator for up to 3 days.

Grilled Zucchini with Mediterranean Sauce

Preparation Time: 15 minutes Servings 4

NUTRITION: 132 Calories; 11.1g Fat; 4.1g Carbs; 3.1g Protein; 1.3g Fiber

INGREDIENTS

- 1 pound zucchini, cut lengthwise into quarters
- 1/2 teaspoon red pepper flakes, crushed
- Salt, to season
- 1/4 cup extra-virgin olive oil
- 1 teaspoon garlic, minced

For the Sauce:

1. 1 tablespoon fresh scallions, minced
2. 1 tablespoon fresh basil, chopped
3. 1 teaspoon fresh rosemary, finely chopped
4. 3/4 cup Greek-style yogurt

DIRECTIONS

1. Begin by preheating your grill to a medium-low heat.
2. Toss the zucchini slices with the olive oil, garlic, red pepper, and salt. Grill your zucchini on a lightly-oiled grill for about

10 minutes until tender and slightly charred.

3. Make the sauce by whisking all of the sauce Ingredients.

4. Storing

5. Place the zucchini in airtight containers or Ziploc bags; keep in your refrigerator for 3 to 5 days.

6. Place the sauce in airtight containers; keep in your refrigerator for 3 to 5 days.

7. Place the zucchini in a freezable container; they can be frozen for up to 10 to 12 months.

8. Bake the thawed zucchini at 200 degrees F until they are completely warm. Serve with the sauce on the side. Enjoy!

Keto Noodles with Oyster Mushroom Sauce

Preparation Time: 15 minutes Servings 4

NUTRITION: 85 Calories; 3.5g Fat; 6.4g Carbs; 5.8g
Protein; 3.3g Fiber

INGREDIENTS

- 2 zucchinis, cut into thin strips
- 2 tablespoons olive oil
- 1 yellow onion, minced
- 2 garlic cloves, minced
- 1 pound oyster mushrooms, chopped
- 1 cup pureed tomatoes
- 1 cup vegetable broth
- 1 teaspoon Mediterranean sauce

DIRECTIONS

1. Parboil the zucchini noodles for one minute or so. Reserve.

2. Then, heat the oil in a saucepan over a moderately-high heat. Sauté the onion and garlic for 2 to 3 minutes.

3. Add in the mushrooms and continue to cook for 2 to 3 minutes until they release liquid.

4. Add in the remaining Ingredients and cover the pan; let it simmer for 10 minutes longer until everything is cooked through.

5. Top your zoodles with the prepared mushroom sauce.

6. Storing

   7. Place your zoodles in airtight containers or Ziploc bags; keep in your refrigerator for 3 to 5 days.

   8. Place your zoodles in a freezable container; they can be frozen for up to 10 to 12 months. Bake the thawed zucchini at 200 degrees F until they are completely warm. Enjoy!

Autumn Eggplant and Squash Stew

Preparation Time: 35 minutes Servings 6

NUTRITION: 113 Calories; 7.9g Fat; 3.7g Carbs; 2.8g Protein; 2.2g Fiber

INGREDIENTS

- 2 tablespoons olive
- 2 garlic cloves, finely chopped
- 3 ounces acorn squash, chopped
- 1 celery, chopped
- 2 tablespoons fresh parsley, roughly chopped
- Sea salt and pepper, to taste
- 1/2 teaspoon ancho chili powder
- 2 tomatoes, pureed
- 2 tablespoons port wine
- 1 large onion, chopped
- 3 ounces eggplant, peeled and chopped

DIRECTIONS

1. In a heavy-bottomed pot, heat olive oil over a moderately-high heat. Sauté the onion and garlic about 5 minutes.
2. Add in the acorn squash, eggplant, celery and parsley;

continue to cook for 5 to 6 minutes.

3. Add in the other Ingredients; turn the heat to a simmer. Continue to cook for about 25 minutes.

4. Storing

5. Spoon the stew into airtight containers; keep in your refrigerator for up to 3 to 4 days.

6. For freezing, place the stew in airtight containers or heavy-duty freezer bags. It will maintain the best quality for about 5 months. Defrost in the refrigerator. Enjoy!

Vegetables with Spicy Yogurt Sauce

Preparation Time: 45 minutes Servings 4

NUTRITION: 357 Calories; 35.8g Fat; 5.2g Carbs; 3.4g Protein; 2.5g Fiber

INGREDIENTS

- 1/4 cup olive oil
- 1/2 teaspoon garlic, sliced
- 1/2 pound broccoli, cut into sticks
- 2 celery stalks, cut into sticks
- 2 bell peppers, deveined and sliced
- 1 red onion, sliced into wedges
- For the Spicy Yogurt Sauce:
- 1 ½ cups Greek-Style yogurt
- Salt and pepper, to taste
- 2 tablespoons mayonnaise
- 1 poblano pepper, finely minced
- 1 tablespoon lemon juice

DIRECTIONS

1. Toss the vegetables with olive oil and garlic. Arrange your vegetables on a parchment-lined baking sheet.

2. Roast in the preheated oven at 380 degrees F for about 35 minutes, rotating the pan once or twice.

3. Thoroughly combine all Ingredients for the sauce.

4. Storing

5. Place the roasted vegetables in airtight containers or Ziploc bags; keep in your refrigerator for up to 3 to 5 days.

6. Place the spicy yogurt sauce in airtight containers or Ziploc bags; keep in your refrigerator for up to 3 to 5 days.

7. To freeze, arrange the roasted vegetables on a baking sheet in a single layer; freeze for about 2 hours. Transfer the frozen fries to freezer storage bags. Freeze for up to 12 months. Bon appétit!

Cheesy Italian Pepper Casserole

Preparation Time: 1 hour Servings 4

NUTRITION: 408 Calories; 28.9g Fat; 4.6g Carbs; 24.9g Protein; 3.5g Fiber

INGREDIENTS

- 8 Italian sweet peppers, deveined and cut into fourths lengthwise
- 6 whole eggs
- 1/2 cup Greek-style yogurt
- 3/4 pound Asiago cheese, shredded
- 1 leek, thinly sliced
- 1/2 teaspoon garlic, crushed
- Sea salt and ground black pepper, to taste
- 1 teaspoon oregano

DIRECTIONS

1. Arrange the peppers in a lightly greased baking dish.
2. Top with half of the shredded cheese; add a layer of sliced leeks and garlic. Repeat the layers.
3. After that, beat the eggs with the yogurt, salt, pepper, and

oregano. Pour the egg/yogurt mixture over the peppers. Cover with a piece of foil and bake for about 30 minutes.

4. Remove the foil and bake for a further 10 to 15 minutes.

5. Storing

6. Slice the casserole into four pieces. Divide the pieces between airtight containers; it will last for 3 to 4 days in the refrigerator.

7. For freezing, place each portion in a separate heavy-duty freezer bag. Freeze up to 2 to 3 months. Defrost in the microwave or refrigerator. Bon appétit!

The Best Keto Pizza Ever

Preparation Time: 25 minutes Servings 4

NUTRITION: 234 Calories; 16.1g Fat; 6.3g Carbs; 13.6g Protein; 3.6g Fiber

INGREDIENTS

For the Crust:

- 1/4 cup double cream
- 1 tablespoon olive oil
- 1 pound cauliflower florets
- 1/2 cup Colby cheese
- 4 medium-sized eggs
- Salt and pepper, to taste

For the Topping:

- 1 tomato, pureed
- 1/2 cup green mustard
- 1 tablespoon fresh basil
- 1/4 cup black olives, pitted and sliced
- 1 cup mozzarella cheese

- 1/2 cup romaine lettuce

- 1 cup lollo rosso

DIRECTIONS

1. Parboil the cauliflower florets in a large pot of salted water until it is crisp-tender; add in the cheese, eggs, cream, olive oil, salt, and pepper.

2. Press the crust mixture into the bottom of a lightly oiled baking pan. Bake in the middle of the oven at 385 degrees F. Bake

    for 13 to 15 minutes or until the crust is firm.

3. Storing

4. Place the cauliflower crust in airtight container or heavy-duty freezer bags; keep in the refrigerator for a week.

5. For freezing, place the cauliflower crust in a heavy-duty freezer bag; freeze up to 3 months. Defrost in your microwave for a few minutes.

6. Top with the other Ingredients, ending with the mozzarella cheese; bake until the cheese is bubbly and hot. Bon appétit!

Oven-Baked Avocado

Preparation Time: 25 minutes

Servings 6

NUTRITION: 255 Calories; 21g Fat; 3.3g Carbs; 10.8g
Protein; 4.8g Fiber

INGREDIENTS

- 3 medium-sized ripe avocados, halved and pitted
- 3 ounce Pancetta, chopped
- 2 eggs, beaten
- 3 ounces chive cream cheese
- Salt and pepper, to taste

DIRECTIONS

1. Begin by preheating an oven to 380 degrees F. Place the avocado halves in a baking pan.
2. Thoroughly combine the eggs, cheese, Pancetta, salt, and pepper. Spoon the mixture into avocado halves.
3. Bake in the preheated oven for 18 to 20 minutes.
4. Storing
5. Place the stuffed avocado in airtight containers; keep in your refrigerator for 3 to 4 days.

Cauliflower and Oyster Mushroom Medley

Preparation Time: 20 minutes

Servings 4

NUTRITION: 300 Calories; 27.9g Fat; 8.6g Carbs; 5.2g Protein; 2.6g Fiber

INGREDIENTS

- 1/2 head cauliflower, cut into small florets
- Salt and pepper, to taste
- 2 tablespoons Romano cheese, grated
- 10 ounces Oyster mushrooms, sliced
- 2 garlic cloves, minced
- 1/2 stick butter, room temperature
- 1/3 cup cream of celery soup
- 1/3 cup double cream
- 1/4 cup mayonnaise, preferably homemade

DIRECTIONS

1. In a saucepan, melt the butter over a moderate heat. Once hot, sauté the cauliflower and mushrooms until softened.
2. Add in the garlic and continue to sauté for a minute or so or until aromatic.

3. Stir in the cream of celery soup, double cream, salt, and pepper. Continue to cook, covered, for 10 to 12 minutes, until most of the liquid has evaporated.

4. Fold in the Romano cheese and stir to combine well.

5. Storing

6. Divide your medley between four airtight containers or Ziploc bags. Refrigerate for up to 3 days.

7. For freezing, place your medley in four Ziploc bags and freeze up to 6 months. Defrost in your refrigerator or microwave. Serve with mayonnaise and enjoy!

Japanese-Style Eringi Mushrooms

Preparation Time: 15 minutes Servings 3

NUTRITION: 103 Calories; 6.7g Fat; 5.9g Carbs; 2.7g Protein; 3.3g Fiber

INGREDIENTS

- 8 ounces Eringi mushrooms, trim away about 1-inch of the root section
- Salt and Sansho pepper, to season
- 1 ½ tablespoons butter, melted
- 1 cup onions, finely chopped
- 2 cloves garlic, minced
- 2 tablespoons mirin
- 1/2 cup dashi stock
- **1 tablespoon lightly toasted sesame seeds**

DIRECTIONS

1. Melt the butter in a large pan over a moderately-high flame. Cook the onions and garlic for about 4 minutes, stirring continuously to ensure even cooking.
2. Add in the Eringi mushrooms and continue to cook an additional 3 minutes until they are slightly shriveled.
3. Season to taste and add in the mirin and dashi stock;

continue to cook an additional 3 minutes.

4. Storing

5. Place the Eringi mushrooms in airtight containers; keep in your refrigerator for 3 to 5 days.

6. Place the Eringi mushrooms on the parchment-lined baking sheet, about 1- inch apart from each other; freeze for about 2 to 3 hours.

7. Remove the Eringi mushrooms to a freezer bag for long-term storage; they will maintain the best quality for 10 to 12 months. Garnish with sesame seeds. Enjoy!

Mediterranean Creamy Broccoli Casserole

Preparation Time: 25 minutes Servings 3

NUTRITION: 195 Calories; 12.7g Fat; 6.7g Carbs; 11.6g
Protein; 3.2g Fiber

INGREDIENTS

- 3/4 pound broccoli, cut into small florets
- 1 teaspoon Mediterranean spice mix
- 2 ounces Colby cheese, shredded
- 3 tablespoons sesame oil
- 1 red onion, minced
- 2 garlic cloves, minced
- 3 eggs, well-beaten
- 1/2 cup double cream

DIRECTIONS

1. Begin by preheating your oven to 320 degrees F. Brush the
   sides and bottom of a casserole dish with a nonstick
   cooking spray.

2. In a frying pan, heat the sesame oil over a moderately-high
   heat. Sauté the onion and garlic until just tender and
   fragrant.

3. Add in the broccoli and continue to cook until crisp-tender for about 4 minutes. Spoon the mixture into the preparade casserole dish.

4. Whisk the eggs with double cream and Mediterranean spice mix. Spoon this mixture over the broccoli layer.

5. Bake in the preheated oven for 18 to 20 minutes.

6. Storing

7. Slice the casserole into three pieces. Divide the pieces between three airtight containers; it will last for 3 to 4 days in the refrigerator.

8. For freezing, place each portion in a separate heavy-duty freezer bag. Freeze up to 2 to 3 months. Defrost in the microwave or refrigerator.

9. Top with the shredded cheese and broil for 5 to 6 minutes or until hot and bubbly on the top. Bon appétit!

Healthy Waffles

Preparation Time: 10

minutes Cooking Time: 10

minutes Serve: 4

Ingredients:

- 8 drops liquid stevia
- 1/2 tsp baking soda
- 1 tbsp chia seeds
- 1/4 cup water
- 2 tbsp sunflower seed butter
- 1 tsp cinnamon
- 1 avocado, peel, pitted and mashed
- 1 tsp vanilla
- 1 tbsp lemon juice
- 3 tbsp coconut flour

Directions:

1. Preheat the waffle iron.
2. In a small bowl, add water and chia seeds and soak for 5 minutes.
3. Mash together sunflower seed butter, lemon juice, vanilla, stevia, chia mixture, and avocado.
4. Mix together cinnamon, baking soda, and coconut flour.

5. Add wet ingredients to the dry ingredients and mix well.

6. Pour waffle mixture into the hot waffle iron and cook on each side for 3-5 minutes.

7. Serve and enjoy.

Nutritional Value (Amount per Serving):

- Calories 220

- Fat 17 g

- Carbohydrates 13 g
- Sugar 1.2 g

- Protein 5.1 g

- Cholesterol 0 mg

Cheese Zucchini Eggplant

Preparation Time: 10

minutes Cooking Time: 2

hours Serve: 8

Ingredients:

- 1 eggplant, peeled and cut in 1-inch cubes
- 1 ½ cup spaghetti sauce
- 1 onion, sliced
- 1 medium zucchini, cut into 1-inch pieces
- 1/2 cup parmesan cheese, shredded

Directions:

1. Add all ingredients into the crock pot and stir well.
2. Cover and cook on high for 2 hours.
3. Stir well and serve.

Nutritional Value (Amount per Serving):

- Calories 47
- Fat 1.2 g
- Carbohydrates 8 g
- Sugar 4 g
- Protein 2.5 g
- Cholesterol 2 mg

Coconut Kale Muffins

Preparation Time: 10
minutes Cooking Time: 30
minutes Serve: 8

Ingredients:

- 6 eggs
- 1/2 cup unsweetened coconut milk
- 1 cup kale, chopped
- ¼ tsp garlic powder
- ¼ tsp paprika
- 1/4 cup green onion, chopped
- Pepper
- Salt

Directions:

1. Preheat the oven to 350 F.
2. Add all ingredients into the bowl and whisk well.
3. Pour mixture into the greased muffin tray and bake in oven for 30 minutes.
4. Serve and enjoy.

Nutritional Value (Amount per Serving):

- Calories 92
- Fat 7 g
- Carbohydrates 2 g

☐ Sugar 0.8 g

☐ Protein 5 g

☐ Cholesterol 140 mg

Kohlrabi with Garlic- Mushroom Sauce

Preparation Time: 15 minutes Servings 4

NUTRITION: 220 Calories; 20g Fat; 5.3g Carbs; 4g Protein; 3.8g Fiber

INGREDIENTS

- 3/4 pound kohlrabi, trimmed and thinly sliced
- 1/2 pound button mushrooms, sliced
- 1 ½ cups sour cream
- 3 tablespoons olive oil
- 1/2 cup white onions, chopped
- 1/2 teaspoon garlic, chopped
- Kosher salt and ground black pepper, to taste

DIRECTIONS

1. In a large pot of salted water, place the kohlrabi and parboil over medium-high heat for about 8 minutes. Drain.

2. In a saucepan, heat the oil over medium- high heat. Sauté the onions, mushrooms, and garlic until they've softened.

3. Season with salt and pepper to taste. Add in the sour cream and stir to combine well.

4. Storing

5. Transfer the vegetables to the airtight containers and place in your refrigerator for up to 3 to 5 days.

6. For freezing, place the vegetables in freezer safe containers and freeze up to 8 to 10 months. Defrost in the microwave for a few minutes. Bon appétit!

Greek-Style Vegetables

Preparation Time: 15 minutes

Servings 4

NUTRITION: 318 Calories; 24.3g Fat; 5.1g Carbs; 15.4g Protein; 1.7g Fiber

INGREDIENTS

- 1/2 pound brown mushrooms, chopped
- 1 cup broccoli, cut into small florets
- 1 medium-sized zucchini, chopped
- 8 ounces feta cheese, cubed
- 1 teaspoon Greek seasoning mix
- 2 tablespoons olive oil
- 1 onion, chopped
- 1 teaspoon garlic, minced
- 1 vine-ripened tomato, pureed
- 1/4 cup white wine

DIRECTIONS

1. In a medium pot, heat the oil over a moderately-high heat. Sauté the onion and garlic for about 5 minutes, adding a splash

of water if needed, until tender and aromatic.

2. Add in the mushrooms, broccoli, zucchini, Greek seasoning mix, tomato puree, and white wine. Continue to cook for 4 to 5 minutes or until they've softened.

3. Storing

4. Place the Greek vegetables in airtight containers or Ziploc bags; keep in your refrigerator for 3 to 5 days.

5. Place the Greek vegetables in freezable containers; they can be frozen for up to 10 months. Defrost in the refrigerator or microwave. Serve with cubed feta cheese. Enjoy!

. Easy Keto Broccoli Pilaf

Preparation Time: 20 minutes Servings 4

NUTRITION: 126 Calories; 11.6g Fat; 5.4g Carbs; 1.3g Protein; 2.7g Fiber

INGREDIENTS

- 1 head broccoli, broken into a rice-like chunks
- 1 Italian pepper, chopped
- 1 habanero pepper, minced
- 1/2 shallots, chopped
- 1/2 teaspoon garlic, smashed
- 1 celery rib, chopped
- 1/2 stick butter
- Salt and pepper, to your liking

DIRECTIONS

1. In a saucepan, melt the butter over a moderately-high heat. Saute the shallot, garlic, and peppers for about 3 minutes.
2. Stir in the broccoli and celery; continue to cook for 4 to 5 minutes or until tender and aromatic. Season with salt and pepper to taste.
3. Continue to cook for 5 to 6 minutes or until everything

is cooked through.

4. Storing

5. Spoon the broccoli pilaf into four airtight containers; keep in your refrigerator for 3 to 5 days.

6. For freezing, place the broccoli pilaf in airtight containers or heavy-duty freezer bags. Freeze up to 10 to 12 months. Defrost in the microwave. Bon appétit!